# ·THE·
# HORSE SHOEING
## BOOK
## A Pictorial Guide for Horse Owners and Students

'It's very sad—this used to
be a tyre and exhaust centre
before all the car thefts'

# ·THE·
# HORSE SHOEING
## BOOK
## A Pictorial Guide for Horse Owners and Students

**MARTIN HUMPHREY** BVMS, MRCVS, AWCF

J. A. ALLEN · LONDON

**British Library Cataloguing-in-Publication Data.**
A catalogue record for this book is available from the British Library.

ISBN 0.85131.617.4

Published in Great Britain in 1995 by
J. A. Allen & Company Limited,
1 Lower Grosvenor Place, Buckingham Palace Road,
London, SW1W 0EL

Illustrations by Maggie Raynor
Typographic design by Paul Saunders
Layout by Dick Vine
Edited by Jane Lake

Typeset by Setrite Typesetters Ltd., Hong Kong
Printed by Bath Press Ltd, England

*To John Hickman*

# CONTENTS

# ACKNOWLEDGEMENTS

Thanks to: Anthony Bailey; Barbara Davis; Carol Ryan; Caroline Burt; Katie Davis; Jan Reed; Jane Lake; Maggie Raynor; Martin Pipe; Robert Lemieux; Robert Oliver; Sallie Walrond; Stephen Hadley; Tom Ryan; Vivienne.

Cover photographs are from the Museum of English Rural Life, Anthony Cain and Martin Humphrey. The photograph on page 91 of Sallie Walrond was taken by Peter Higby of P.H. Photography, 15 Fen Lane, Pott Row, Kings Lynn, Norfolk. The photographs on pages 101 and 102 were provided by the Museum of English Rural Life, University of Reading, Reading, Berkshire.

# PREFACE

This book is intended for all. I have used everyday terms, not always the correct scientific terms. I have not tried to cover everything to do with horses and shoeing but to give an insight into what has often seemed to be a mysterious craft. For further and more detailed reading you should consult *Hickman's Farriery*, also published by J.A. Allen.

*Martin Humphrey*

# CHAPTER 1

# THE NEED FOR SHOEING

The most important parts of a horse are its four hooves. Horses, and their close relations the donkeys and zebras, are distinguished from other animals by having one hoof per limb.

Cows, pigs and sheep have two, and human beings have five 'hooves' for each limb, our fingernails and toenails.

The hoof is a hard outer layer inside which is living flesh, blood and bone. A hoof is made of horn and forms a natural slipper for the horse to walk in. Like a fingernail it is dead tissue and can be cut or filed without pain.

Wild horses take plenty of exercise because they live on wide open plains and are always on the move. Hooves are worn down as fast as they grow and so are always the right length. With hooves in good shape a wild horse moves quickly and can outrun predators such as the big cats. Horses are specially designed for running and can reach a top speed of 65 kph (40 mph) over a short distance.

A horse needs to have strong feet. If it cannot stay mobile it cannot survive in the wild. From the time when horses were first caught and domesticated by man the importance of good feet has been recognised. Shoeing was invented because even the best-footed horses would become footsore when travelling long distances or carrying heavy loads.

*Wild horses.*

If a riding horse or pony has good feet and is kept off the roads for most of the time it may not need to be shod. Like a wild horse its feet will naturally stay at the right length while hoof growth and wear are equal.

Horses which work regularly on the roads without shoes would wear their hooves away quickly. Their feet would become sore. A shoe protects the hoof from wearing away. Most riding horses must be shod or they would go lame.

Apart from ponies, most breeds of horse do not have strong enough hooves for working unshod, even when ridden off the road. Modern horses tend to have relatively large bodies and small feet that are easily bruised by uneven or stony ground. A shoe protects the foot from bruising as well as from wear.

Shoes allow a horse to keep working in comfort. They are also often useful for horses who are retired or used for breeding whose feet become sore and need protecting.

Horses kept in fields hardly wear their hooves at all. In fact the hooves can grow too long and impair the animal's movement. The hooves must be trimmed to keep them short and tidy.

If the hooves are not strong they may become deformed in shape and are liable to split and crack. Small stones also tend to work into the bottom of the hooves. This all leads to discomfort for the horse. To keep such weak hooves in good shape they must be carefully trimmed and shod.

Hooves grow continually, shod or unshod. Shoes must be taken off every month for the hooves to be cut back. If this is not done the hooves will grow too long causing strain to the limb. The hooves are often ready for trimming before the shoes have worn thin, in which case the shoes can be used

Shod horses on the road.

A horse with overgrown hooves.

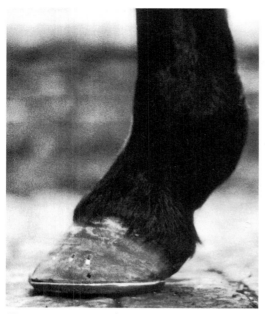

*Hooves grow too long.*

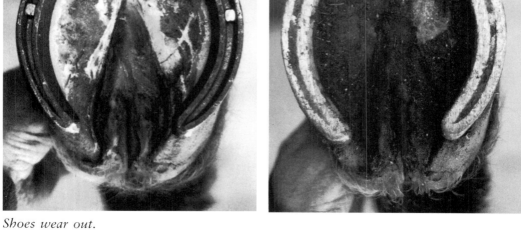

*Shoes wear out.*

again. When the same shoes are put back on again they are called removes or refits.

All shoes will wear out in time and need to be renewed.

Different varieties of horse require different styles of shoeing. The shoeing needs of an event horse differ from those of a racehorse, and a shire pulling a wagon will have different shoeing needs from those of a show pony.

Shoes can be modified to help horses cope with problems of conformation, disease or injury. There are an infinite variety of surgical shoes, each of which may be right for any one horse at any one time.

Whatever the horse and whatever its shoeing regime its feet need daily care and maintenance.

When buying a horse your budget must allow for regular visits from the farrier. Neglecting regular attention to a horse's feet, whether shod or not, can easily cause problems which can be hard to correct. The old saying 'no foot no horse' is as true as ever.

The farrier has an important position in the horse world. He or she is indispensible, someone we cannot do without. Fortunately today's farriers are better trained and educated than ever before. To get the best out of your farrier you should understand something of the craft of farriery.

*Farrier Reg Brown in Chorleywood, Hertfordshire, 1994.*

# CHAPTER 2

# THE HOOF AND FOOT

The hoof and the foot are commonly talked about as if they
are the same thing. Strictly speaking they are not the same.
The hoof is just the outer horny layer. The foot is the hoof
plus all the important structures inside it.

## The Hoof

A hoof has several parts.

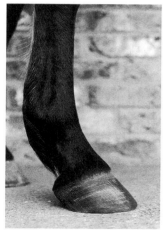

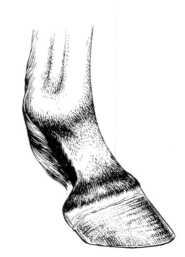

*Side view of the hoof.*

The hoof wall is what you see when the foot is on the ground. It is the fingernail of the horse and is the strongest part of the hoof. It can be trimmed and cut just as our own fingernails can. The hoof wall is about 1 cm ($\frac{1}{2}$ in) thick. A horseshoe can be nailed to it without any injury to the animal.

The top of the hoof where it joins the skin is called the coronet. The wall grows from the coronet towards the ground. The rate of growth is about 8 mm ($\frac{5}{16}$ in) every month. At this rate it takes about a year to grow a whole new hoof.

The periople is the soft rim of horn at the coronet. It covers and protects the junction of the hoof wall and the skin. The hoof wall is the horse's fingernail and the periople is the cuticle.

The wall at the front is called the toe. At the back it is called the heels and the parts of the wall at each side where nails are placed are called the quarters. Toe, quarters and heels are not different features, they are just names for different areas of the same thing, the hoof wall.

Dark hooves are thought to be tougher than white hooves but this is much less important than the general size, shape and thickness of the hooves. A good hoof has thick straight walls and a concave sole. Horses with weak deformed walls and flat soles have bad conformation and should not be bought.

*Growth rings.*

*Laminitis rings.*

Rings around the hoof are common and represent variations in the horn growth. Normal growth rings or 'grass rings' are parallel to each other and to the coronet. Rings which are further apart at the heels than at the toe are not normal. They are laminitis rings and show that the horse has had laminitis, a common and sometimes crippling disease.

Lifting up the hoof we see the wall running around the outside.

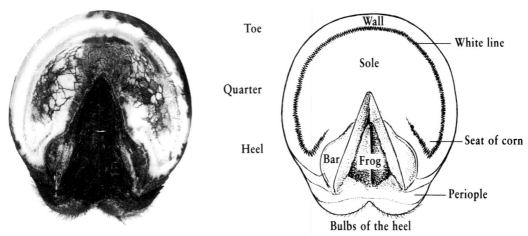

*The hoof, ground surface.*

In the middle is the sole. At the back is the frog. The sole and frog do not take much weight: the hoof wall carries most of the weight of the horse. The sole and frog are both made of horn but are softer and weaker than the wall.

The frog is a kind of pad and being flexible and squashy it helps to absorb shock and to give the horse grip. The frog has three grooves or clefts, one in the centre and one on each side. It is important to keep these grooves free of dirt and stones.

The bars are formed by the wall turning inwards and forwards at the heels.

The area of the sole at each heel is called the seat of corn.

The white line is the name given to the junction between the wall and sole. Nails must not enter the sole, only the wall, therefore nails must not pass inside the white line. The white line marks the position of the laminae inside the hoof.

The hoof normally has an angle of about 55 degrees. Every horse has its own individual hoof conformation. Hind hooves are usually a little more upright than fore hooves.

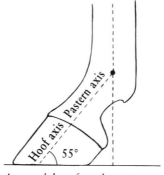

*A good hoof and pastern.*

The most important consideration is that the hoof and pastern are aligned when a horse is standing square so that movement in the pedal joint will not be restricted when the horse moves.

# Bones

The knee of the horse is similar to the human wrist and altogether different from the human knee. The horse's equivalent joint to the human knee is the stifle.

A horse's forelimb below the knee is a modified hand with just one finger. The fetlock is similar to a knuckle and the pastern and foot are the horses finger. As in a finger there are three main bones below the fetlock: the long and short pastern bones and the pedal bone. There is also the tiny navicular bone.

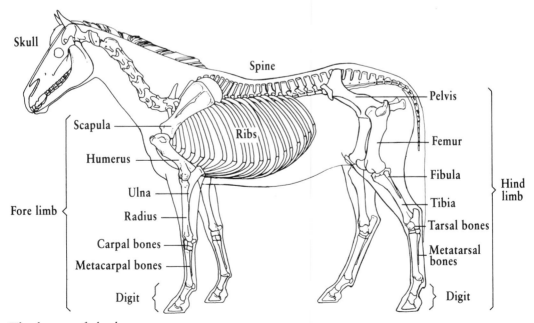

Skull

Spine

Pelvis

Scapula

Ribs

Femur

Humerus

Fibula

Ulna

Tibia

Radius

Tarsal bones

Carpal bones

Metatarsal bones

Metacarpal bones

Fore limb

Hind limb

Digit

Digit

*The bones of the horse.*

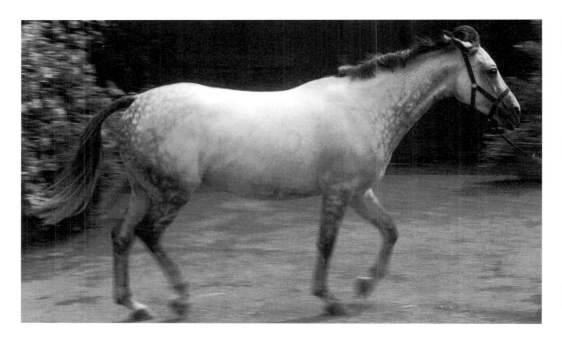

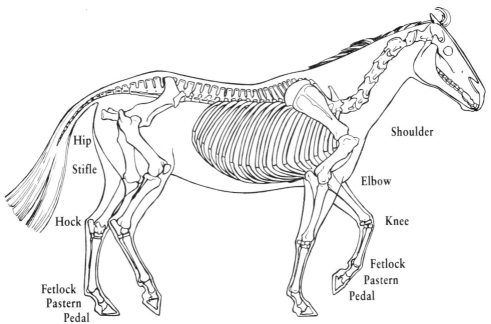

*The limb joints of the horse.*

# Joints

There are three joints in and near the foot. Joints are made where bones meet and allow movement to take place. The ends of the bones are protected by a thin layer of smooth cartilage and lubricated by an oily joint fluid. Ligaments keep the joints in place, holding the bones together and resisting movement in the wrong direction.

The fetlock joint has a great deal of movement. It sinks as the horse takes weight on it. This is an important way for the horse to absorb shock although it puts a great strain on the tendons at the back of the limb.

The pastern joint is between the two pastern bones. It has very little movement and is rarely a site of lameness except for occasionally a form of arthritis known as ringbone.

The pedal joint is inside the hoof. It also has a great deal of movement. The pedal joint is made between the short pastern bone and the pedal bone.

# The Navicular Bone

The navicular bone is a small bone which lies between the pedal joint and the deep flexor tendon. It is subject to a lot of pressure and wear owing to its position and if it becomes damaged and painful the horse will show signs of the lameness known as navicular disease.

# Cartilages

The cartilages of the foot can be felt above the coronet on either side. They are normally flexible and help to give the foot shape and pliability. If the cartilages turn to bone the horse is said to have sidebones. The foot becomes less flexible and the horse is more prone to lameness.

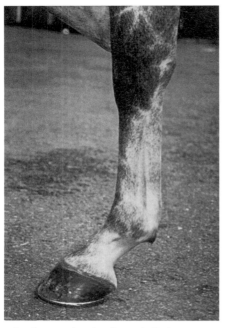

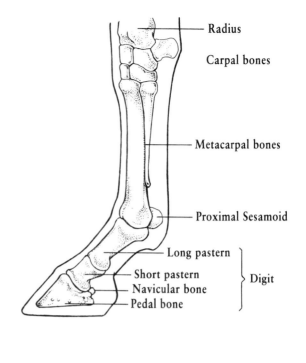

- Radius
- Carpal bones
- Metacarpal bones
- Proximal Sesamoid
- Long pastern
- Short pastern
- Navicular bone
- Pedal bone

} Digit

*The lower forelimb and digit.*

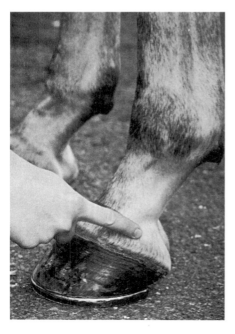

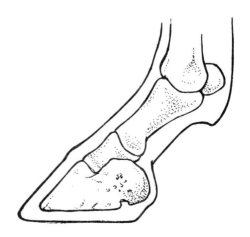

*The hoof cartilages. These are in pairs, attached to either side of the pedal bone.*

# Laminae

The laminae are the attachments between the hoof wall and the pedal bone. The horny insensitive laminae on the internal surface of the hoof wall dovetail with the fleshy sensitive laminae on the outer surface of the pedal bone. The pedal bone hangs from the laminae inside the hoof. All the weight of the horse goes through them. Laminitis is inflammation of the laminae.

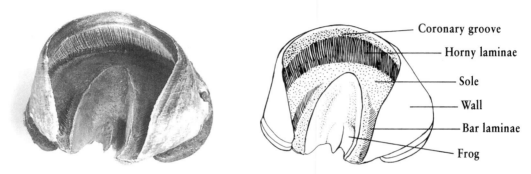

*The horny laminae and the inside of the hoof.*

# Tendons

A horse moves by the action of its muscles. Muscles are situated in the upper limb and act on the joints of the lower limb through connecting tendons. If the muscles pull when the limb is off the ground the limb will move. If the muscles pull while the limb is on the ground then the body will move.

The important tendons of the limbs are the flexor tendons which come from muscles below the elbow and stifle. They run down the back of each limb and attach to the foot and pastern. They flex the joints to lift the feet up. They also support the limb when it is on the ground and takes weight. They are put under a great deal of strain and injuries to the tendons are all too common, especially when horses are overexerted.

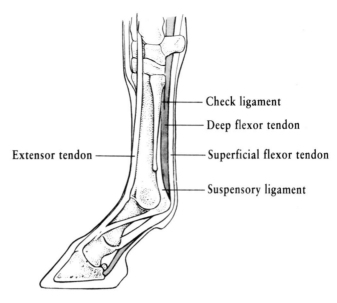

Check ligament

Deep flexor tendon

Extensor tendon

Superficial flexor tendon

Suspensory ligament

*The tendons.*

# Conformation

All horses have the same number of bones, muscles and other biomechanical parts, but they are not all put together in the same way. The way a horse is put together is called its conformation. Good conformation means that all the parts of the horse work harmoniously, weight is borne evenly, and shocks and stresses are absorbed comfortably. Poor conformation means that some part of the body will endure excessive strain. Just as a chain is only as strong as its weakest link, so the usefulness of a horse is limited by the weakest point in its structure.

Poor conformation may lead to poor performance or to injury.

A common conformation fault is turned out toes. This puts more strain on the inside of the limb and foot. Splints and corns are often the result. The opposite problem is turned in toes, commonly called pigeon-toes. A pigeon-toed horse suffers

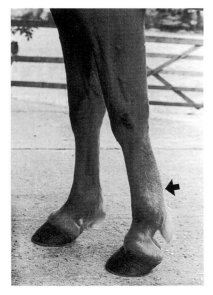

*Strained tendon.*

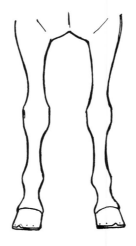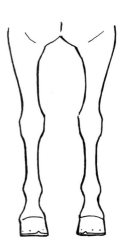

*Splay feet and pigeon toes.*

from strain on the outside of the limbs and feet. It will wear the outsides of its shoes heavily and may suffer from sidebone or ringbone.

Unlevel feet and shoes can make a horse appear to have bad conformation when it does not, or at least make things look worse than they are. By the same token a crafty farrier can sometimes disguise faults and make a horse look better than it is.

Trimming the hoof is possibly the most important part of the shoeing process. How a hoof is trimmed and shaped will probably have more effect on the horse's balance and movement than the type of shoe or how it is fitted. It needs a good eye and also a good knowledge of horse conformation and movement.

If poor conformation is inherited it may be impossible to prevent or correct. However many problems can be corrected at an early age if detected in time.

## FOOT CONFORMATION

A normal hoof has a slope of about 55 degrees.

BOXY FEET These are upright feet with an angle of more than 55 degrees. They are not always regarded with favour by horse owners but many vets and farriers believe that boxy feet are a good thing. If they are steeper than 60 degrees they are called club feet. Club feet are abnormal and usually result from flexural deformity (see Chapter 6) in early years or from tendon shortening due to injury. Quite often only one foot is affected. Whether or not a horse is sound with a club foot depends on how severe the abnormality has become.

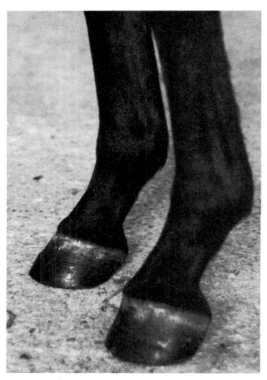

*A good foot and a club foot.*

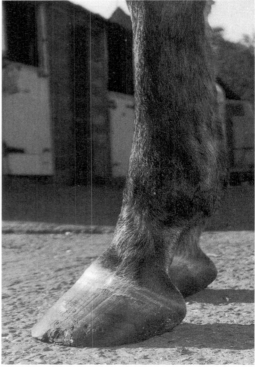

*A flat foot. The hoof pastern axis is broken back.*

**FLAT FEET** It is common in older books to see 45 degrees given as a normal hoof angle. In fact this is now considered to be an abnormally sloping foot shape. A horse with an angle of less than 50 degrees will have a flat sole and weak heels. It will be very susceptible to bruising and puncture wounds of the sole and may also be prone to navicular disease and tendon strain.

**HOOF PASTERN AXIS** The correct hoof angle for any individual horse is when the hoof has the same slope as the pastern. As long as the hoof pastern axis is not broken back or forward then the pedal joint will be able to move freely and the foot will not be put under undue strain.

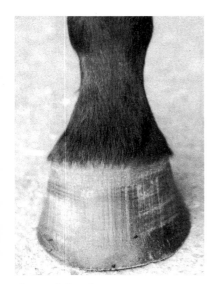 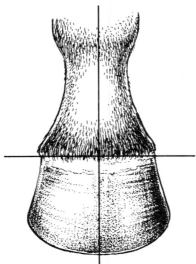

*A good hoof.*

**WRY FEET** When you look at a horse from the front its feet should be symmetrical. If one side is longer or more sloping than the other side then it has lost its symmetry and is a wry foot. This can be caused by neglect, if trimming has been overlooked, or it can be associated with angular deformity of

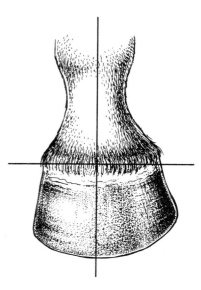

*Wry feet.*

the limb. If a limb is not straight then the foot will not meet the ground correctly and will become irregularly shaped as a result. In such a case a wry foot should be accepted as natural.

## Breeding

Everyone seems to appreciate that good feet are one of a horse's most important attributes but, when it comes to breeding, it seems that quality of foot is often overlooked. Natural selection does not come into play in domestic horse breeding; in practice it is unsound mares which are more often used for breeding, many with foot problems which could be inherited by their offspring. As a result horses' feet seem to be getting weaker.

# CHAPTER 3

# THE HORSESHOE

## Shoe Structure and Basic Types

A horseshoe is simply a bar of steel which is bent to the shape of the hoof and nailed to it.

### PLAIN STAMPED SHOE

This is a simple type of horseshoe.

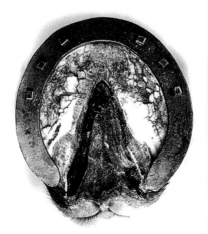

*A plain stamped shoe.*

The nails must not go into the sole. The shoe is made and fitted so that the nail holes are over the white line. This means that the nails will pass through the full thickness of the wall, giving a good hold without damaging any sensitive parts of the foot.

The plain stamped shoe is a perfectly good shoe for all types of horses, but over the years many variations have evolved for different uses.

## FULLERED AND CONCAVE SHOES

It was found that better grip was obtained if a groove was put in the shoe. The groove is called fullering.

It was also discovered that the inside of the shoe could be sloped to continue the concave shape of the sole of the hoof. This gives even more grip and makes the shoe lighter.

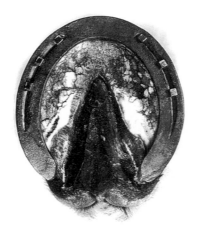

*A fullered shoe.*                    *A concave shoe.*

A combination of concaving and fullering gives the most grip.

Although these shoes do not wear as well as plain stamped shoes they are the best shoes for riding across country and are especially popular for hunting.

*A concave fullered shoe.*     *The foot surfaces are the same for most shoes.*

All these changes are to the ground surface. The foot surface is the same for all these shoes. It is nearly always flat. The only common alterations to the foot surface are rolling the toe and seating out.

*A seated-out shoe.*

When steel bar started to be produced already concaved and fullered it saved the farrier a great deal of labour and became universally used for most types of horses. Only carthorses are still shod with plain stamped shoes as a rule because concave fullered bar is not made in a large enough size.

A shoe is described as having a toe, quarters and heels just like the hoof. Clips are thin triangular projections drawn from the edge of the shoe which help to steady the shoe against the hoof. Commonly one clip is used at the toe of front feet and two clips are drawn, one either side of the toe, on hind feet.

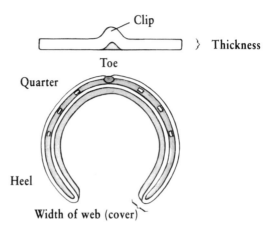

*Parts of the shoe.*

The width of the metal is called the web. The width of web used for each horse will depend on the size and thickness of its hooves. As a rule the wider the web the better it is for the horse as the shoe will support and protect more of the hoof.

*Narrow web shoe.*          *Medium web shoe.*          *Wide web shoe.*

## ALUMINIUM SHOES

Shoes can be made of aluminium instead of steel. These are most popular for racehorses. It is said that an ounce of weight off the foot is worth a pound off the back, in other words the lighter the shoes the faster the horse can run. The trouble with aluminium shoes is that they have to be fitted cold (they lose hardness once they have been heated) and they wear out very quickly. Aluminium shoes are often called plates.

*Aluminium alloy shoes.*

# Horseshoe Nails

Horseshoe nails are specially made for the purpose. They come in a range of different sizes to suit all sizes of horse and pony.

*Horseshoe nail.*

Horseshoe nails have flat sides so they fit into the square nail holes in the shoe.

They have a sharp point to ensure they go through the hoof easily. The point has a bevel on it making certain that the nails do not go in a straight line but turn outwards when driven. This means that they must be put in the right way round so that the point will not turn inwards and prick the sensitive foot.

The head of the nail is tapered so that it can be countersunk into the full thickness of the shoe and does not loosen as the shoe wears through.

*A nail in a shoe.*

Horseshoe nails, like the shoes, are made from mild steel.

Special nails are made for racehorses. They have a small head which is specially designed to fit into the fullering of thin light aluminium racing shoes.

*Plate nails.*

# Keeping a Grip

Even concave fullered shoes do not give very good grip either on roads or off them and so many ways of improving the holding of shoes have been tried.

Calkins are the oldest way of getting extra grip. The heels of the shoes are turned down into a block. Calkins cannot be used on the front feet because they would cause a horse to injure its elbows when lying down.

*Calkins.*

*Calkin and wedge.*

Because the inside calkin sometimes hits the other limb when horses travel at speed the inside calkin is often rounded to make a wedge.

A wedge and calkin do not give very good grip on the roads and for many years many inventive and bizarre ways of getting grip were tried such as corrugated shoes, shoes with rope inserts and many kinds of rubber pad.

Only with the use of tungsten carbide, also known as borium, has a satisfactory solution been found. Tungsten carbide is a very hard metal. When incorporated into a shoe the softer steel wears away around the tungsten carbide which sticks out to give a strong grip. It is easier not to insert the tungsten directly but as part of a steel stud, plug or non-slip nail hammered into a hole in the shoe.

Road studs or plugs should not protrude far. They should, as near as possible, be flush with the shoe so as not to upset the balance of the foot.

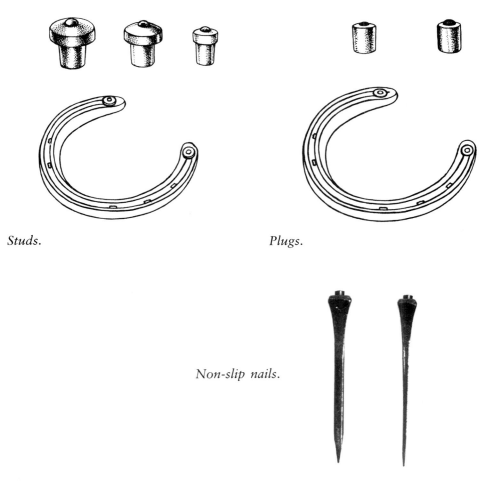

Studs.                                    Plugs.

Non-slip nails.

If slipping is very bad then tungsten carbide crystals can be welded to the surface of a shoe. This gives really excellent grip

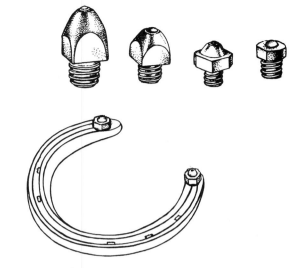

*Tungsten carbide (borium) applied to the outside heel of a hind shoe.*

*Screw-in studs.*

and also stops the shoe from wearing away. However it can cause jarring on the limbs. A small amount of sliding as the feet hit the ground is thought to help in reducing concussion.

If better grip off-road is needed screw-in studs are the best solution. A hole is punched or drilled into the shoe and the hole is threaded so that a stud can be screwed into it when required and removed afterwards. There are many varieties of stud for different sizes of horses and different conditions of the ground.

Studs should be selected that will sink fully into the ground, otherwise they will unbalance the foot. As a rule the smallest studs that you can get away with should be used, and they should be used in pairs, one in each heel of the shoe. Pointed studs are for hard ground, square studs for soft ground.

Screw in studs should be removed after work. The stud holes can be plugged with cotton wool to keep out dirt and grit which can make it hard to get the studs back in again.

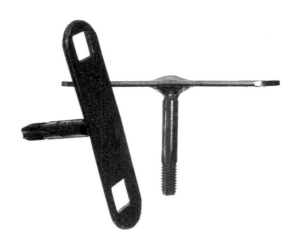

*T taps.*

A T tap is used to keep the thread of the stud hole clear and to remove any burring around the hole. The handle of the T tap is a spanner for tightening and untightening the studs.

As the shoes wear down the depth of the stud hole is reduced. Studs should not be screwed in when the shoes have worn thin because they will press into the foot and cause lameness. Studs should only be used for grip and not to prevent uneven shoe wear.

# CHAPTER 4

# TAKING SHOES OFF AND PUTTING SHOES ON

## Taking Off a Shoe

Although every rider should be able to take off a loose shoe in an emergency it is not always an easy or safe procedure. It needs care and is physically awkward to do. When your horse is being shod ask your farrier to show you how it is done.

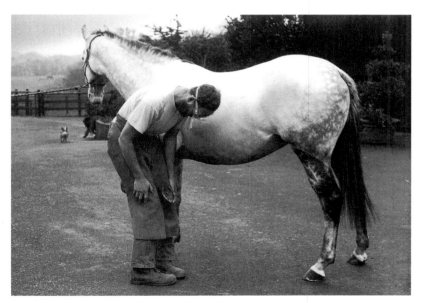

*The horse's forelimb is held between the farrier's legs.*

A book is no substitute for practical experience. However if you understand the principles it will be easier to cope.

A farrier will wear protective clothing and have the proper tools for the job. Additionally he will ensure that the working area and conditions are suitable and safe.

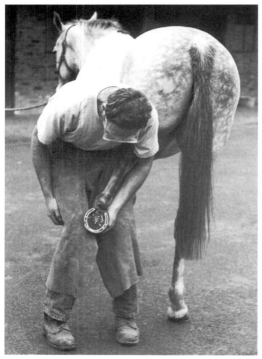

*To take off a hind shoe the farrier rests the hind limb on his lap.*

*ABOVE RIGHT: First the clenches are straightened with hammer and buffer.*

*CENTRE RIGHT: The pincers are closed fully under one heel and the shoe levered away from the hoof.*

*RIGHT: The same is done at the other heel. If the pincers are not closed fully the jaws will press into the horse's sole and cause discomfort.*

*The pincers are moved forwards along each side in turn to lever the shoe further away.*

*Finally the shoe is pulled off at the toe.*

The essential tools for taking off a shoe are hammer, buffer and pincers. Stout boots, a leather apron and eye protection are desirable. Loose clothing should be avoided.

Before starting, the foot should be clean and dry and be picked out carefully.

## Putting On a Shoe

This can only, at the time of writing, legally be performed by a registered farrier or by a veterinary surgeon.

A good shoe is an extension of the hoof. The hoof will grow into the shoe. The overall appearance will be natural and pleasing.

The frog is trimmed as necessary.

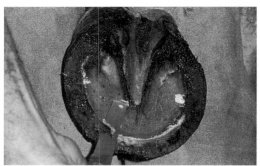

Excess sole is removed. This is usually just the loose flakes that have not been shed; very little in this case. Many people worry that a flaky sole is a problem but it is a normal feature of a good thick sole that the outer layers start to crumble.

The hoof wall is trimmed with hoof cutters. The cut should not go beyond the level of the sole.

The wall is levelled with the coarse side of the rasp, then the file side. It is quite a skill to be able to get a level surface.

When the right shoe has been made it will be easy to fit to the shape of the hoof. This shoe is still hot. It is kept hot in the forge fire for the fitting process because the shoe is then easier to alter in shape. This is called hot shoeing.

*The shoe is cooled.*

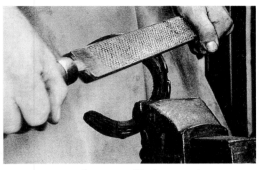

*Any sharp edges are filed smooth.*

*The shoe is nailed on using a light hammer.*

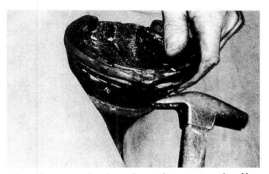

*The sharp end of each nail is twisted off using the claw of the hammer so that if the horse snatches its limb away it will not injure the farrier or its own limbs.*

*Nail pullers can be used to remove a nail that has come out in the wrong place.*

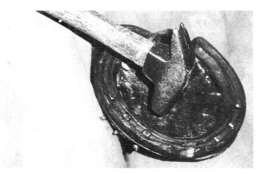

When all the nails are in place they are tapped firmly down into the shoe.

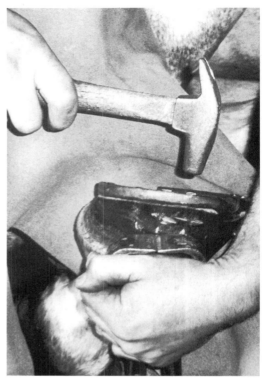

The nail heads are tapped with the pincers held under the nail stubs which bends the stubs over. The horse's limb is now brought forwards and the foot rested on the farrier's knee or on a stand to be finished off.

The nail stubs are filed short with the file side of the rasp. The rasp is also used to file a little hoof away under each nail so that the finished clench will be flush with the hoof.

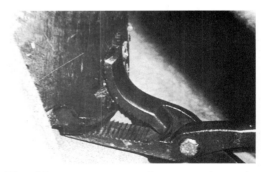

Clenching tongs are used to turn the stubs down and bed them into the hoof to make the clenches.

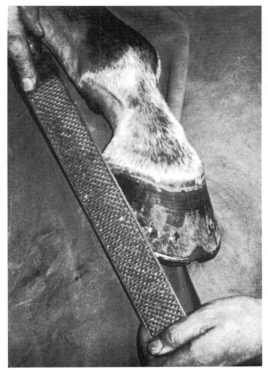

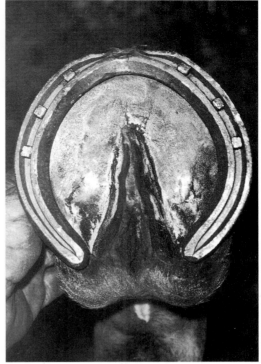

The clenches and the hoof are lightly filed smooth.

A good shoe covers the wall to each heel. The toe clip is in the centre, in line with the frog.

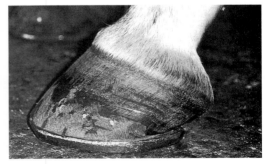

The shoe conforms to the outline of the hoof so that no more than a little wall is overhanging and needs to be rasped off. The shoe should project slightly from under the hoof towards the heels to allow for growth and expansion. There are no gaps between the shoe and the hoof. The nails are well up the wall into sound horn. The clenches are strong and in a neat line.

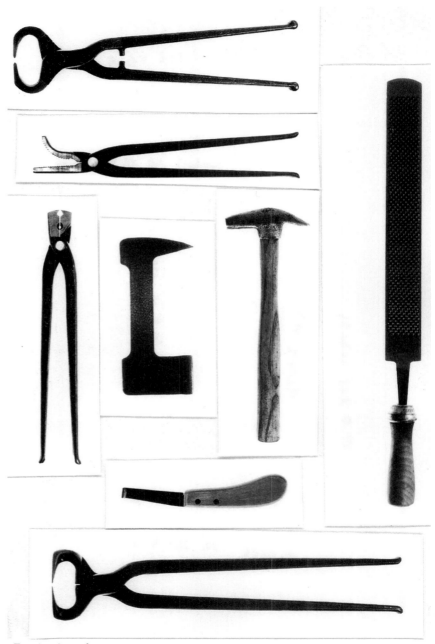

*Farriers' tools.*

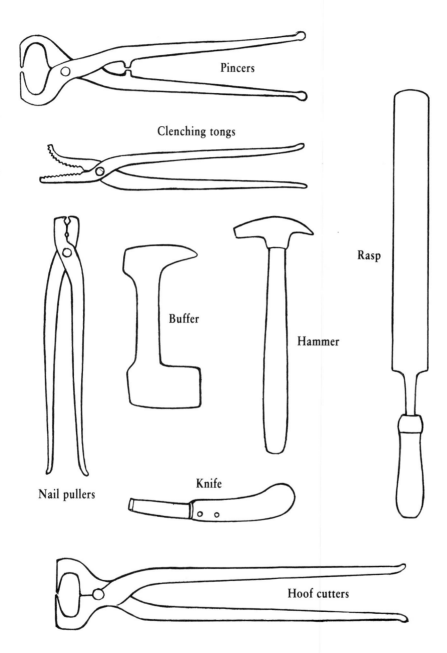

Pincers

Clenching tongs

Rasp

Buffer

Hammer

Nail pullers

Knife

Hoof cutters

*Farriers' tools.*

# Cold Shoeing

Ready-made shoes can be fitted cold and when done well the results can be very satisfactory. It is a method that has arisen out of convenience over the years in that it allows horses to be shod in their stables. This makes it easy for the owner and gives the farrier shelter. It also tends to be quicker and thus cheaper. Some farriers use a conventional anvil to shape shoes cold but others use a variety of improvised anvils ranging from specially made 'stall jacks' to tripods or short lengths of railway sleeper.

*Colin Smith FWCF (Hons) at the forge, 1994*

# CHAPTER · 5

# SURGICAL SHOES

We expect a lot from our horses but very few horses are perfect. Shoes may need to be modified to help a horse to move comfortably or to alleviate a medical condition.

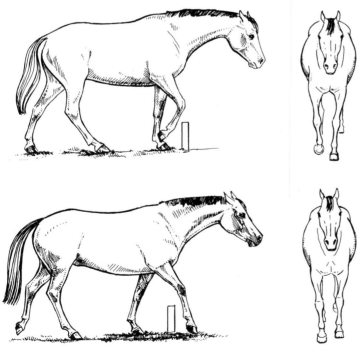

*The walk.*

*The walk (continued)*

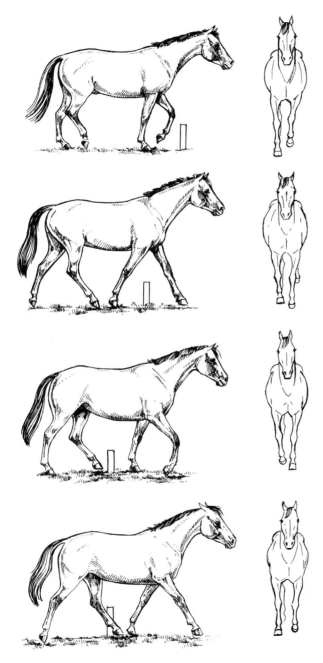

*The trot.*

# Movement

The way a horse moves depends mainly upon its conformation. Movement can also be altered by other factors such as unlevel feet, injury, lack of fitness or the influence of the rider.

A sound horse with good conformation and balanced feet will move its limbs in alignment with its body.

**WINGING OUT** The foot swings away from the body and then back again as it goes forwards. This is common when horses have toe-in conformation. Also known as paddling or dishing.

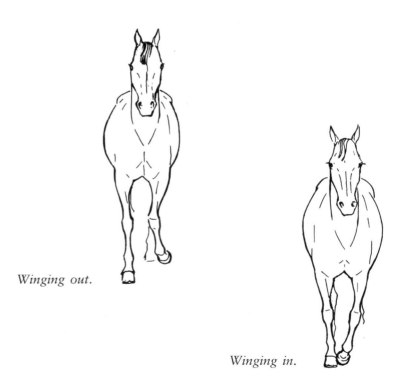

*Winging out.*

*Winging in.*

**WINGING IN** The foot comes in under the body and then goes back again as it moves forwards. This happens with toe-out conformation. Also called winging.

**KNEE ACTION** Excessive bending (flexion) of the limbs is seen in Hackneys and Morgans. The knees are lifted very high. This is partly a natural gait for these breeds but it is exaggerated by using heavy shoes and by letting the toes grow very long. Any horse which is too long in the toe, wearing heavy shoes or perhaps sore in its feet will show a lot of knee action.

*The high knee action of the Hackney.   The long stride of a show pony.*

**EXTENSION** Show ponies, for example, are expected to have a long, gliding, almost floating step. This is helped by wearing light shoes or no shoes at all.

# Lameness

Lameness is an unevenness of movement caused usually by pain. It can also be found in the absence of pain where there are mechanical or nerve problems.

Soundness is a measure of an animal's usefulness. A horse which is lame is unsound. An unsound horse is not necessarily lame however. Horses can be considered to be unsound for many other reasons such as heart or eye problems.

Severe lameness is apparent to anyone, for the horse will not put the injured limb to the ground. Such dramatic lameness is fortunately rare. Usually a horse will be only slightly lame and detection becomes more difficult.

*A very lame horse will not put its foot to the ground.*

Front limb lameness is best seen when the horse is being led towards you. The horse shows that it is lame by nodding its head down when the good limb hits the ground and lifting its head when the lame limb comes to the ground.

*This pony is lame in its right forelimb.*

Hind limb lameness is much harder to detect. It is best seen when the horse is led away from you. The quarter on the lame side will sink more than the quarter on the sound side.

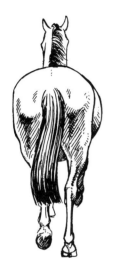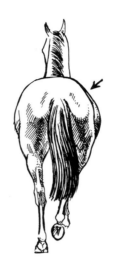

*This horse is lame in its right hind limb.*

The trot is the best gait for detecting lameness. This is because, when trotting, all the weight goes onto one front limb and one hind limb, whereas at the walk there are three limbs on the ground at any one time. A horse which is only slightly lame will look sound at the walk but the lameness will show up at trot.

Some lameness is so slight that it will only show when the horse is ridden at the trot in a circle. Even then the horse may be sound on one type of surface but not on another.

Sometimes lameness may be present in more than one limb. Examining horses to find the cause of lameness can be very difficult. It can happen that the cause is never found even after the most exhaustive examinations.

Most lamenesses are in the foot. A veterinary surgeon will always examine the foot very carefully when searching for the cause of lameness.

Any sign of heat or a strong pulse in the fetlock or pastern area will point towards the foot as the source of pain. If the suspicion is that the lameness is in the foot the vet may remove the shoe and search the foot with hoof testers and a hoof knife.

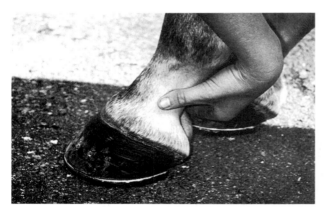

*Feeling the pulse.*

*Using hoof testers.*

## Surgical Shoes

Surgical shoes are called by a variety of names such as corrective, orthopaedic, pathological, remedial, surgical and therapeutic shoes. They all mean more or less the same thing.

An understanding of normal feet and shoeing will not go very far when dealing with surgical shoeing. Special veterinary knowledge is needed and close co-operation between farrier and vet is very important for a successful outcome.

Surgical shoes should not be applied 'off the peg' but with a clear understanding of what the problem is, what needs to be done, what the shoe will do and how it should be fitted, as well as what are the possible pitfalls.

There are so many different kinds of shoe it is impossible to show them all. However, many of the most well known are as follows.

## ROLLED TOE SHOE

A rolled toe shoe is designed to help a horse lift its foot more easily. It reduces the strain on the tendons and the navicular bone. It is a simple aid to many horses with lameness problems. It is also often used to prevent stumbling. Some farriers believe in shoeing all horses with rolled toes.

*Rolled toes.*

## SEATED-OUT SHOE

A seated-out shoe has the upper surface relieved so that it does not press on the sole of the foot. This is necessary for horses which do not have the normal cup shape of the sole. They may be naturally flat-footed or may have dropped soles due to laminitis. As pressure on the sole can be very painful to a horse this can be a very valuable shoe to use.

*A seated-out bar shoe.*

## WEDGE HEELS

When a hoof is too sloping the tendons and navicular bone can be put under additional strain. By raising the heels of the shoe a better hoof angle is created which immediately relieves the strain. It lifts the frog off the ground and can cause extra pressure on the heels of the hoof however. A bar or pad that spreads the weight onto the frog helps to avoid compressing weak heels.

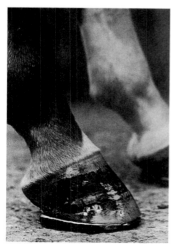

*A graduated shoe.*

*A spavin shoe.*

*A shoe with a plastic wedge.*

A shoe that is thicker at the back is the old fashioned method of raising the heels and there is nothing wrong with it. Care must be taken that in fitting the shoe hot the thick heels of the shoe do not burn away too much horn.

A lighter and more labour saving method is to use plastic wedges between a normal shoe and the foot. These also help to absorb some concussion and prevent bruising.

## EXTENSIONS

Extending the heels of a shoe backwards is thought to reduce the strain on the tendons and the navicular bone. It is currently a more popular method than raising the heels with wedges. Because the angle of the hoof is left low it is necessary to roll the toe as well.

*Heel extensions.*

Extending the toe of a shoe forwards will increase strain on the tendons and is used when the muscles and tendons have contracted due to disease and need to be stretched. It is not something to be undertaken without veterinary supervision.

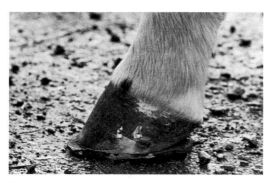 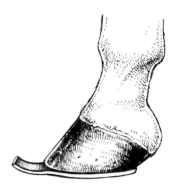

*Toe extensions.*

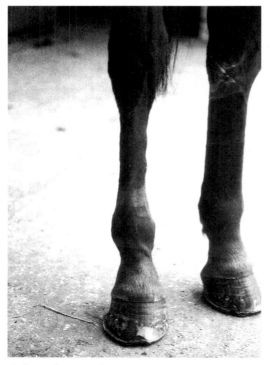 

*A lateral extension.*

Extending a shoe sideways alters the way a horse places its foot on the ground. An extension on the outside (lateral side) makes it difficult for the horse to bring the foot under its body and makes it place the foot out more. A lateral extension shoe would be used for a horse which brings its feet too close together. This might mean that its limbs hit each other or that it wears the outsides of its shoes excessively or that it does not feel correct when ridden. Such a problem is more common in the hind limbs.

An extension on the inside (medial side) makes it harder for the horse to place its foot away from its body. It would be used for a horse whose feet are too far apart. This is more common in the front limbs, especially in foals whose limbs are developing an angular deformity.

## TRAILERS

A trailer or 'donkey heel' is a heel extension which turns outwards. Used only on the outside heel of a hind foot, for safety reasons, it works like a lateral extension.

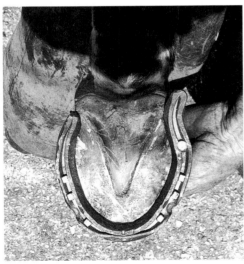

*A trailer.*

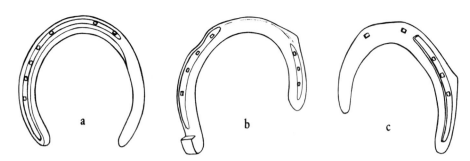

*Brushing shoes: a) feather-edged shoe for heel brushing (a light concave fullered fore shoe); b) three-quarter shoe for heel brushing (a concave fullered hind shoe with calkin); c) three-quarter shoe for toe brushing (a part fullered hind shoe).*

## BRUSHING SHOES

Brushing is a form of interference where a horse moves its limbs too closely and hits itself.

Brushing shoes were a big thing in the past and all the old horse books are full of descriptions of different types of shoes to prevent brushing. Perhaps horses really did brush more in the old days than now. It may have been the different road surfaces and the long working hours that made horses tired and caused them to knock their limbs together more.

Nowadays brushing is uncommon. Often brushing will occur in a young, green or out of condition horse and will disappear as the horse gets fitter, stronger and better schooled. The same is true for other forms of interference such as forging and over-reaching.

Brushing shoes generally do more harm than good. This is because the nails are not evenly distributed, the shoes do not support the whole hoof wall, and they may unbalance the horse. When a horse does brush it needs to be watched carefully and the farrier should be able to modify the shoeing so as to correct the problem. Usually this will involve only minor adjustments to the way the hooves are trimmed and shod. Lateral extension shoes or trailers will often prevent brushing.

## OVER-REACHING SHOES

Over-reaching can be a considerable nuisance. An over-reach is when a hind foot hits the back of a front foot. When a hind shoe hits the bulb of the front heel it can cause a nasty wound. If the hind shoe misses the bulb of the heel but catches the heel of the front shoe then the front shoe will often be pulled off. An over-reaching shoe is a graduated hind shoe with a concave toe.

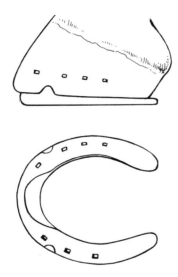

*Over-reaching shoe.*

## BAR SHOES

A bar shoe is a shoe with a bar joining the two heels. Thus the shoe makes a complete ring. The shape of the bar varies with its purpose.

The traditional bar shoe has the heels joined with a straight bar. Thus it does not protrude at the back. It is used for horses with corns to shift weight from the affected heel to the other heel and to the frog.

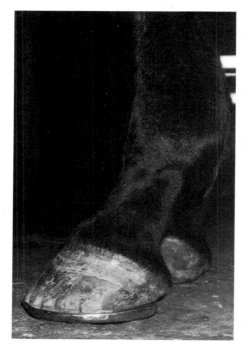
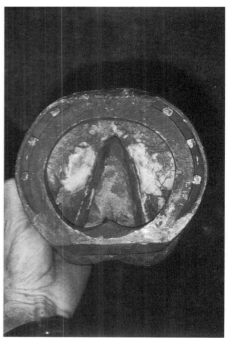

*A bar shoe on a normal foot and on a damaged hoof.*

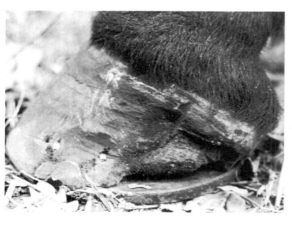

An egg bar shoe is a shoe with a round or oval shape. The bar continues the curve of the shoe and protrudes backwards under the bulbs of the heels. It does not usually rest on the frog, rather coming behind it. It is used in the same way as a shoe with extended heels, to reduce strain on the tendons and on the navicular bone.

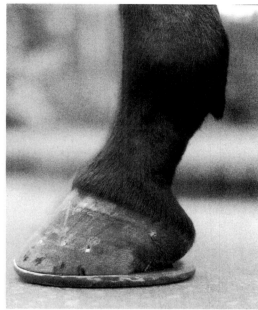

*An egg bar shoe.*

The heart bar shoe has recently been in vogue after being promoted as a treatment for horses with laminitis. By pressing towards the front of the frog which overlies the pedal bone it is claimed to stabilise the bone within the hoof. It has had mixed results. Applying a heart bar shoe to a horse's foot is potentially dangerous and should only be performed under veterinary direction.

The patten bar shoe is an old design of shoe which is still useful today. Its other name is the rest shoe because it is designed to rest a limb after a tendon injury. A horse must be

*A heart bar shoe.*

*A patten bar shoe.*

confined to a stable when wearing one of these shoes and so is certain to get rest in one way or another. The patten shoe should not be left on for more than a few weeks or the injured tendon will heal in a shortened and contracted condition.

The rocker bar is another old shoe which is little used today. It was intended for horses with ringbone, an arthritic condition where joint movement is reduced. Horses are no longer kept working with the sort of joint conditions where a shoe like this would be of help.

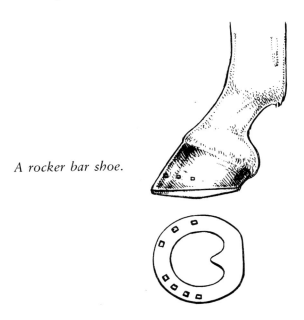

*A rocker bar shoe.*

## SPRINGTOPS

These are a French invention, first introduced into the UK in 1990. They are made of a light aluminium alloy and are very different from the conventional horseshoe as they cover the entire sole. Not only do they cover the sole but they put weight onto it which in theory is quite the wrong thing to do. However they do seem to help some horses with lameness problems such as ringbone and are something to consider when other shoeing methods have failed.

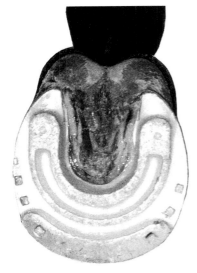

*Springtop.*

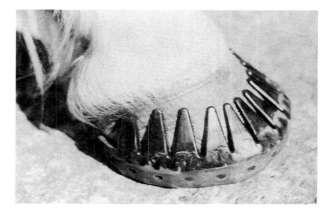

*A glue-on shoe.*

## GLUE-ON SHOES

Horseshoeing has changed relatively little over hundreds of years. Much effort has recently gone into finding alternatives to nailing on metal shoes. Whoever does come up with a cheap and effective alternative technology will no doubt expect to make a fortune.

Glueing on plastic shoes has become a practical alternative in recent years and there are several different types of glue-on shoe available. However, all are significantly more expensive than ordinary shoes.

The present range of glue-on shoes do not stay on as long or wear as well as traditional shoes. At the time of writing their use is restricted to special situations. I find them particularly useful for young foals with limb deformities that need surgical shoeing. It could well be that as the technology improves they will come more into everyday use.

# CHAPTER 6

# FOOT CARE FOR HORSES
# NOT IN WORK

## Brood Mares

Brood mares vary a great deal in the conditions in which they are kept. Some are much loved members of the family, but others are valued only for the foals they produce and are often overlooked as individuals deserving of care and attention.

Brood mares divide their time between two managements, at home and at the stud, and consequently no-one is clearly responsible for the state of their feet. Add the fact that the care is often delegated by owners to employees and it is no surprise that brood mares often have very neglected feet.

Carrying the extra weight of a foal puts an extra strain on a mare's limbs and feet and hoof care is especially important. The feet should be cleaned, picked out and inspected daily.

Hind shoes are undesirable in case a mare kicks other horses and causes injury. Most brood mares manage well without hind shoes, but some benefit from wearing shoes on the fore-feet. Shoes will help to prevent the hoof walls from splitting and the soles from getting bruises or puncture wounds. The farrier should attend every four to six weeks to trim the hooves and to refit the shoes if worn.

*Przewalski's wild horses, mare and foal, Equus przewalskii.*

# Foals

Foals should be handled daily and their feet picked up to prepare them for the farrier. If the animal is used to having its limbs and feet handled it will make the farrier's task much easier and safer.

Foals should have their hooves trimmed at one month of age and every month thereafter. This is not just to train the foal, keep the hooves tidy and prevent foot problems, but also in order to detect deformities of the growing limbs.

There are two common kinds of limb deformity in foals.

The joints of a horse bend (flex) by the action of the muscles and tendons of the limb. It sometimes happens that too much tension from the muscles and tendons causes a joint to over bend (contracted tendons).

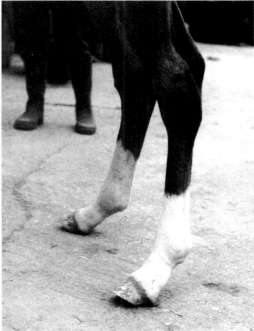

*Contracted tendons.*                    *Weak tendons.*

The opposite can also occur; too little muscle tone causes joints to be overextended.

Such abnormal joint positions are called flexural deformities.

The joints of a horse's limb do not move sideways and so if a limb becomes deformed in a sideways direction it is usually the bones which have bent, generally at the ends where they are most pliable. These are called angular deformities.

Some deformities are present at birth and may well correct themselves quickly, but veterinary advice should always be taken. Some degree of toe-out conformation is normal at 12 months of age and tends to correct itself with time.

Deformities which develop as foals grow are often associated with rapid spurts of growth, and attention to the feeding of the foal is usually required. As the main part of a foal's diet is its

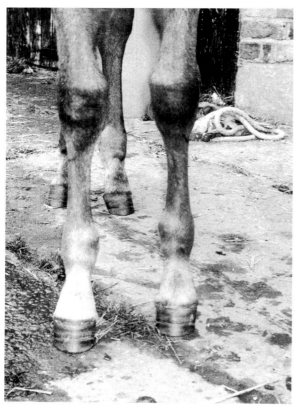

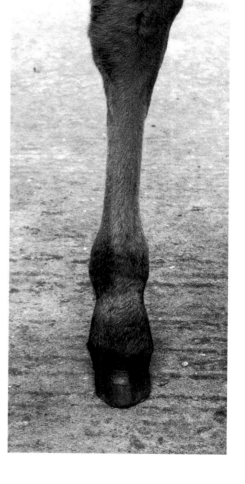

*The left forelimb of a foal bending in from the fetlock.*

*RIGHT: The right hind limb of a foal bending in from the fetlock.*

mother's milk the mare may need to be fed less in order to reduce the richness and quantity of her milk. If possible the foal can be weaned. In addition special shoeing is generally useful if quickly and expertly applied. If shoeing does not bring rapid improvement then surgery is often successful. The golden rule is always to act quickly because as the rate of growth slows and the young tissues become less pliable the conformation becomes more and more fixed.

# Young Stock

The same care that is given to foals should be continued with young stock. Daily handling is just as important because as they get bigger and stronger they can become more awkward and less co-operative. Because they are growing less rapidly they generally need only be attended by the farrier at six-weekly intervals.

*A yearling can be hard to handle.*

Deformities may still develop, especially flexural deformities (contracted tendons), and should be watched for closely. It is very easy to overlook foot deformities when young horses are out in a muddy field; it is important to be extra vigilant.

*Retired to grass, Equus caballus.*

Once a young horse begins work, ordinarily at about four years of age, it will need to be shod. At first usually only a pair of front shoes is fitted. It is surprising how readily most young horses accept shoeing for the first time.

## Retired Horses

Retired horses need a level of general care which should not be underestimated, and it is important that the feet are cleaned, picked out and inspected daily.

As a rule hind shoes are unnecessary and are undesirable when horses are kept in groups because they may kick and injure one another. Many retired horses benefit from being shod on the front feet.

The farrier should attend every six to eight weeks to trim the hooves. It is so easy and so common to delay arranging farrier visits and every effort should be made to make regular appointments. It is especially important to have the horse ready and its feet clean and dry for the farrier when he arrives.

## Donkeys

Donkeys are originally from hot dry conditions. They are not suited to the British climate and their hooves tend to decay owing to the moisture of the ground. They also tend to get insufficient wear because they are rarely worked. Donkeys' hooves should be cleaned and picked out daily, and should be trimmed by a farrier every six to eight weeks. Shoeing is not usually necessary even when a donkey is ridden or driven. Shoeing may be required if the feet are deformed. The complaint is often heard that owners cannot get a farrier for their donkeys, but this is rarely to be believed. Sadly donkeys are often neglected by well-meaning but thoughtless owners.

*A donkey, Equus asinus.*

# Working Horses Without Shoes

If a horse is to go on roads regularly then the hooves will wear down quickly and in no time the horse will be sore. If riding is possible without using the roads then it may be worth considering going without shoes, or perhaps just using front shoes.

Riding without shoes can of course save a lot of money in farriers' bills. There are other advantages too. Unshod hooves grip the ground fairly well and are able to expand better without the restriction of nails. The frog, being nearer to the ground, is able to take more weight and better fulfil its natural functions of shock absorption and of circulating the blood around the foot. The hooves can also wear more easily in the way that is most comfortable to the horse. Furthermore there is less danger to other horses if there is a kicking match.

Unfortunately there are also disadvantages. Without shoes the feet are more susceptible to bruising and puncture wounds. It takes a horse with tough feet to be able to work comfortably. The hooves should have good arched soles; a horse with flat feet will not cope. The bigger a horse and the more weight it has to carry the less successful it will be. A lot may depend upon whether the ground is stony or not.

A horse must also have good conformation to be worked without shoes. If the limbs are not straight the hooves may wear unevenly which will exaggerate the conformation problem and worsen the strains on the bones and joints.

When shoes are removed it will take a few weeks for the hooves to toughen up. Work should be built up slowly and gradually. Lotions that harden the feet can be bought and may help but are unlikely to make a big difference. Some horses which appear to have strong feet are just not comfortable without shoes.

Horses do better without shoes in hot dry conditions than in the wet.

You will still need regular farrier attention to keep the hooves in good shape. The Farriers' Registration Act allows owners to trim hooves but it is definitely a job for an expert and I would not recommend it as a DIY task. After all it is the horse that will suffer if it is not done well.

Normal daily hoof care is even more important of course when a horse is worked unshod.

## Resting Horses Without Shoes

It used to be the custom to turn out all types of working horses for a few months during the summer without shoes. This not only gave them a rest and improved their general condition but gave their hooves a chance to grow without being damaged by nails. This is still the practice with many hunters. If your horse is used less at a particular time in the year then consider whether giving it a holiday without shoes might benefit the horse and the feet. Discuss it with your farrier.

# CHAPTER · 7

# HOOF CARE

## Daily Maintenance

All horses of any age should have their feet cleaned, picked out and inspected at least once a day. This is part of every owner's duty whether or not the horse is stabled or shod. Most problems can then be prevented or are likely to be detected quickly and

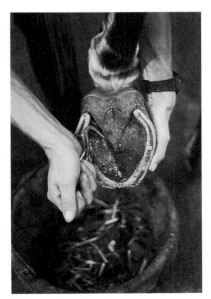

*Using a hoof pick.*

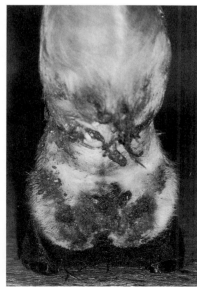

*Mud fever.*

more easily treated. The hooves should also be picked out before and after exercise.

## Problems to Watch

Always be alert for signs of lameness or stiffness.

Limb problems to look out for include cuts and swellings to the limbs, cracked heels and mud fever.

Foot problems include thrush in the frog, foreign matter such as stones, glass or wire trapped in the grooves of the frog or under the shoe, wounds of the coronet, sole or frog, cracks in the wall, and loose shoes or raised clenches.

If in doubt about what to do, call your vet.

## Hoof Oil

Many people paint the hooves with hoof oil after cleaning them. It is usual to pick up the foot and paint the sole and frog as well as the wall.

Hoof oil has the effect of waterproofing the hoof. In wet conditions it tends to prevent the hooves from absorbing too much moisture, and in dry conditions it stops the hooves from losing too much moisture.

The disadvantage of hoof oil is that if the hooves are not clean and dry before it is applied it tends to trap moisture and dirt in the hoof and encourages decay.

Some experts believe that hoof oil does more harm than good. I like to see owners take a pride and interest in their horses' feet and my opinion is that using hoof oil is to be encouraged, as long as it is after shoeing and not before! It is almost as bad to pick up an oily foot as a muddy foot!

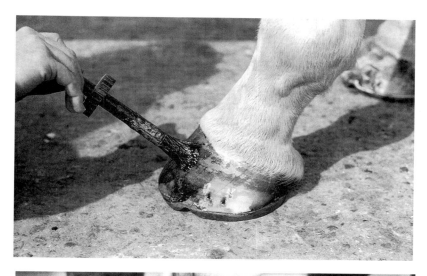

*Oiling a hoof.*

# Brittle Hooves

Brittle hooves have always been a problem. It is usually not a problem to keep shoes on with hot shoeing under good conditions, but it is only natural to want your horse's hooves to

*A brittle hoof.*

look smart without cracks and lumps missing. The more work a horse does the more wear and tear the hooves seem to get, and if the wall does break up badly the shoes will start to press on the sole causing corns and lameness.

## Supplements

Any broken hoof is only a temporary problem because new hoof is growing to replace it all the time. However it does not grow fast enough to please most of us so many products are available which claim to improve hoof growth or quality. Some are added to the diet, others are painted onto the hoof. As a rule I believe that they are a complete waste of time and money because any horse which has a proper balanced diet will not be lacking in any particular ingredient which will affect the hoof. If a horse has been ill and is out of condition then your vet will advise you on what supplements may be required.

# Liniment

The only beneficial treatment for poor hoof growth that I am aware of is to rub liniment into the coronet in order to cause a mild irritation and increase the blood flow to the growing hoof. This may cause a slight increase in the growth of the hoof wall.

# Hoof Hardeners and Conditioners

Hoof hardeners and conditioners are big business because there is such a strong demand from owners for an easy way to improve their horses' feet. A lot of money is spent on advertising products and many extravagant claims are made. If any one of these products came close to doing the things it was said to do then there would be no need for any of the others.

# Thrush

Thrush is a decay of the soft horn of the frog. It usually starts in the central groove. It is commonest in wet conditions and worst in warm weather. It rarely leads to lameness but is smelly and unpleasant and best avoided. A good frog helps the horse's action as it gives grip and absorbs shock as well as promoting the circulation of the blood within the foot.

The grooves of the frog should always be picked out thoroughly with a blunt hoof pick. If there is any sign of dark smelly discharge then the area should be cleaned with antiseptic daily. Ask your farrier to trim away any ragged bits of frog that make cleaning difficult.

*A healthy frog.*

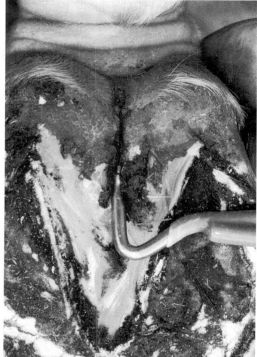

*Thrush.*

## Corns and Bruises

A heavy impact to the horny sole will result in bruising to the sensitive tissues above, usually when the horse treads on a stone. Blood will be released into the deep, new growing horn of the sole. Because of the thickness and opacity of the horny sole the bruising is not visible on external examination and can only be guessed at by the symptoms of lameness, heat and increased pulse in the foot, tenderness in response to hoof testers, and absence of a puncture wound. After about two months have passed there may be blood staining visible in the outer layers of the sole as the horn is replaced and pushed to the surface.

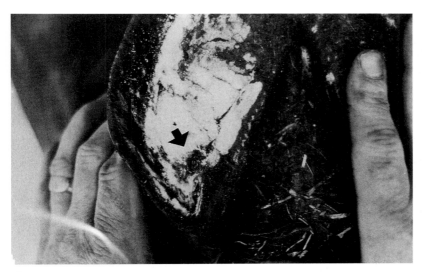

*A corn.*

A bruise in the seat of corn is called a corn. It is not usually caused by an external blow but by pressure against the heel of the shoe. It is particularly likely if the horse has weak hooves, does a lot of work, especially on roads, and if the shoes are ill fitting and have become overgrown by the hoof. A bad corn may become septic and cause an infection.

## Punctured Soles

The sole forms a barrier protecting the delicate tissues within. If the sole is damaged and the barrier broken then dirt and germs get through and cause very painful infections of the foot. Foot injuries tend to be more painful than most other injuries because the horny hoof does not allow room for swelling to take place. This is unfortunate because damaged tissue tends to swell up and the resulting pressure is very painful.

A punctured sole occurs when a horse steps on a sharp object such as a flint or a nail. In most cases the puncture is not deep and responds quickly to treatment. In rare cases where the puncture is very deep and involves the bones, joints or tendons the life of the horse is in serious danger. Punctures can be in the frog as well where they can be harder to find.

# White Line Infection (Gravel)

An infection in the white line can be just as painful as a punctured sole. It can be caused by a small piece of gravel working its way up the white line or just by infection creeping in. The white line is a particularly weak and vulnerable part of the hoof. White line infection can occur in shod and in barefooted horses. If the infection is not drained it will eventually burst out at the coronet.

*A punctured sole.*

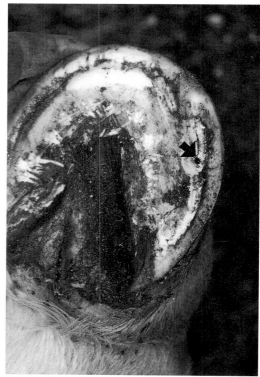

*White line infection.*

# Cracks

Hoof cracks are not uncommon. Many horses have slight flaws running down the hoof which are no more than a thin line. These are never a problem while the hoof is cared for regularly.

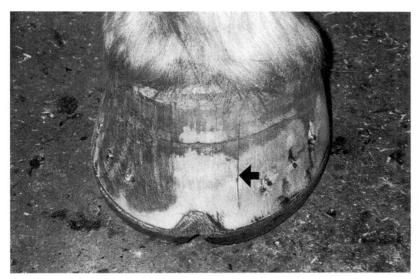

*Minor hoof crack.*

## SANDCRACKS

If hooves are neglected and allowed to grow long then bigger cracks will appear which can cause problems, especially if they extend up to the coronet. Such serious cracks are called sandcracks.

## TRANSVERSE CRACKS

It is also common to see short splits parallel to the coronet which gradually grow down and out of the hoof. These are flaws in the hoof, normally the result of a blow to the coronet and are not often a problem. They can also occur when a hoof infection has travelled up and burst out at the coronet. What-ever the cause they usually grow down and out without causing any difficulties.

*Sandcracks.*

*Transverse hoof crack.*

*Quarter crack.*

## QUARTER CRACKS

Another type of crack is one that appears suddenly due to extreme pressure. These are commonest in race horses. They usually occur in the quarters of the hoof hence their name: quarter cracks. They are painful and may bleed.

## FALSE QUARTER

When a horse has had an injury to the coronet there is usually a scar left behind and the horn produced by that area of the coronet may be abnormal. Sometimes it will form a raised column and there may be a crack present. The hoof here is weak. Because the coronet is permanently damaged the hoof will never again be perfect. The commonest problem is infection getting through to the sensitive tissues beneath. Only if there is a large weak area or an open crack is this likely to be a problem.

*False quarter.*

# Keratoma

A keratoma is a horn tumour. It usually grows on the inside of the hoof wall and presses inwards, wearing a groove in the

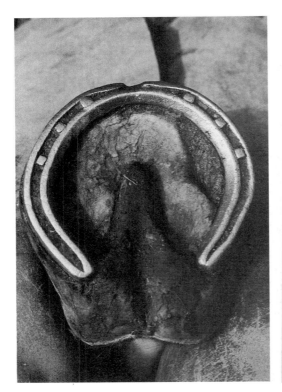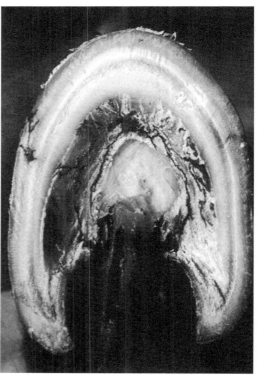

*Keratomas of the hoof wall and of the point of the frog.*

pedal bone. It does not always cause lameness, though if it does then it may be possible to remove it surgically.

# Laminitis

Laminitis is the biggest problem that affects horses' feet today. It is especially common in ponies, but when it does affect a horse it tends to be worse owing to the greater body weight pressing down on the feet. After an attack of laminitis the hoof is deformed and it will take a year for new hoof to grow and replace it. The problem is that often other attacks will occur during this time and the deformity can be prolonged indefinitely in this way. The deformed feet of a laminitis sufferer have flat soles which are very prone to bruising and the animal may be lame for long periods.

Careful and skilled farriery, especially in the trimming of the hoof, can help a great deal but there are no short cuts, easy answers or miracle cures. Most cases will get better as new hoof grows but patience and long term commitment are required.

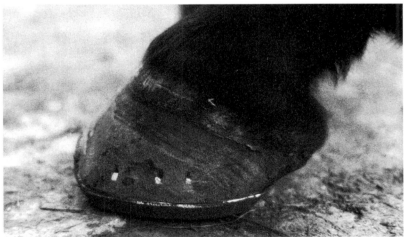

*Laminitis – before and after trimming and shoeing – upright heels would usually be preferred to the sloping heels of the shoe shown here.*

The best cure is prevention. Overfeeding should be avoided and access to rich grass restricted, but exercise is often overlooked and is equally important. After all, horses are fed for the work they do, and a diet that is too much for an idle pony will be just right for a pony that is exercised regularly. Horses and ponies that are kept fit and active day in and day out are much less likely to get laminitis, and after an attack it is better to get a convalescent animal moving about and exercised as soon as is humanely possible.

# CHAPTER 8

# VIEWS ON SHOES

Top horsemen and women give their views on shoeing as they see it.

## Showjumping with Stephen Hadley

*Is shoeing important in showjumping?*

Extremely. The balance of the feet is essential. So many horses come into my yard with total imbalance where previous black-smiths have had a tendency to overtrim either the inside of the foot or the outside. Showjumping is hard on feet, good shoeing helps cushion the blows.

*What type of horse is used in showjumping?*

Mainly half to threequarter Thoroughbred types but a lot more quality has been introduced (mainly from abroad) over the last few years. The plainer horse is now outdated. With so much emphasis on the clock, and distance problems, an athlete is required.

*What shoeing needs does it have?*

Level wearing surfaces. A reasonably short toe and above all a good heel, to reduce jar and forelimb strain. Showjumpers are believed to be more susceptible to navicular disease due to the stress of landing so often; they must have good shock absorbers!

*What are the special demands of showjumping upon shoes?*

Shoes should be reasonably light but hard-wearing. A wide shoe is preferable to a narrow shoe. Most show-jump riders at top level use two large studs per shoe to promote traction. The shoes must not come off very often. Short heels in a shoe are preferable to prevent over-reaching.

*Stephen Hadley.*

*Are there any particular problems you have with shoeing?*

No, not really. Blacksmiths today are very skilful. I hunt a lot of my horses. The odd one can be inclined to lose shoes, which tends to make matters worse because there is not much hoof left to nail to.

*Can shoeing make a difference to your success?*

Obviously. Badly shod horses don't last long. If a horse can land with confidence he will quite simply jump higher and wider and enjoy it for far longer.

*Have you ever had a bad experience with shoes?*

No, I have been very fortunate to have had good blacksmiths throughout my career. I buy and sell a lot of competition horses and hunters these days but I quite simply will not buy bad feet. It is not difficult to shoe a good foot. An expert is needed for a bad one.

*Have you ever had a funny experience with shoes?*

Not really, but my blacksmith always seems to have a fund of funny stories, some of which I would not care to repeat here!

# Eventing with Robert Lemieux

*Is shoeing important in eventing?*

It is probably the single most important element in the management of the event horse. So many problems can be traced back to lack of attention to shoeing.

*What is the typical type of event horse?*

Until recently most have been either full or 7/8 Thoroughbreds. However there is now a proliferation of warmblood crosses which present different shoeing requirements.

*Robert Lemieux.*

*What shoeing needs does it have?*

Taking the full or 7/8 Thoroughbred as typical, care has to be taken, in a lot of cases, not to let the toe become too long causing deterioration of the heel and a lowering of the sole.

*What are the special demands of eventing upon shoes?*

The 'eventing shoe' needs to be all types of shoe in one. It needs to have weight and balance for the dressage and show-jumping phases, to be durable and secure enough for the rigours of cross country, yet able to cope with the speed of the steeplechase like a racing plate! Impossible?

*Are there any particular problems you have with shoeing?*

The majority of blacksmiths are not bold enough with their shaping of the feet. However good the shoes are, if they are put on poorly balanced feet you have problems.

*Do you prefer light shoes?*

I would like to think the event horse could use lighter shoes, but in reality they do not stand up to the demands of the training schedule. If we all changed to competition shoes prior to an event (as in racing) it might be different.

*Have you ever used aluminium or glue-on shoes?*

Only aluminium, and they could not cope with the wear and tear of the conditioning work, especially any roadwork. They simply wore too quickly.

*Do you prefer hot or cold shoeing?*

Hot. I have always felt hot shoeing 'seats' the shoe better and hardens the surface directly beneath the shoe.

*Do your horses wear their shoes out?*

Yes, the toe area is nearly always a problem.

*Can shoeing make a difference to your success?*

In so far as it can affect the total balance of the horse's limbs and thus influence the way in which a horse copes with stress and the distribution of it under the pressure of hard work, yes. Soundness = success.

*Have you ever had a bad experience with shoes?*

I probably missed the '92 Olympic Games due, in part, to the deteriorating balance of my horse's feet throwing pressure onto the high suspensory area. This was a cumulative effect over a period of time.

*Have you ever had a funny experience with shoes?*

At Blenheim three-day-event my horse sprung a shoe on the first circuit of the 'chase. It spun up in the air almost to shoulder level. So I knew exactly where it was, I even saw it the second time around. As I crossed the finish and before the horse had pulled up I jumped off and ran as fast as I could backwards up the 'chase course, dragging my poor horse behind! The supporters waiting for me after the finish thought I had really lost my marbles! The horse had special pads, so I was keen to have the same shoe on again, before the 10 km of tough roads and tracks.

# Driving with Sallie Walrond L.H.H.I.

*Is shoeing important in driving?*

Yes. Vital. On the principle of 'no foot – no horse'. A lot of driven horses are exercised entirely on hard roads and therefore need shoes to prevent the feet from wearing and breaking.

*What is your type of driving horse?*

At present I am driving a five-year-old Connemara which I

*Sallie Walrond.*

have had since he was a yearling. I also drive a 22-year-old home bred part Welsh/Arab/Connemara. I also have a yearling Welsh Section D colt. I work all types of horses and ponies as I teach carriage driving in all of its forms and help people to train and improve their animals so I am quite used to discussing shoeing and foot problems.

*What shoeing needs does it have?*

The Connemara is shod with light concave hunter-type shoes which are removed and replaced about once a month. The old pony is unshod, just trimmed when necessary as she is worked entirely on grass. The yearling will be shod when he is three years old.

*What are the special demands of driving upon shoes?*

Demands vary enormously. I prefer light shoes as I also ride my horses and like to encourage low action. I ride and drive on grass and tracks more than on roads. Also I think that light shoes probably cause less strain and wear to limbs and the horse in general. Some people prefer heavy shoes to encourage extravagant action.

*Are there any particular problems you have with shoeing?*

I have had problems with brittle feet and have pupils who have animals with this problem.

*Have you ever used aluminium or glue-on shoes?*

No, but I have just written to the advertisers about the new 'lightweight' shoes advertised in *Horse and Hound*.

*Do you prefer hot or cold shoeing?*

I marginally prefer hot but for years all my ponies were shod cold and I had no problems. Shoes probably fit better when a horse or pony is hot shod.

*Can shoeing make a difference to your success?*

Yes. From a showing point of view, judges usually look at feet. Speaking as a judge, I am very particular about feet and distrust signs of brittle feet and obvious need for constant shoeing. Also, I am very wary of ill-shaped feet. From a performance angle, I used to have calkins on the outer hind heels and a compensating feather-edged wedge heel on the inner side to give grip on show ring and cross-country surfaces where slopes are negotiated at speed. I also used to use hardened nails behind but *never* in front because of the concussion caused by these.

*Have you ever had a bad experience with shoes?*

Yes, laminitis caused by excessively heavy shoes which had to be used when there was a steel strike. The shoes had had to be imported and my best ever tandem leader got laminitis. Both my blacksmith and my vet assured me that this had been caused by these shoes and *not* by my feeding or mismanagement.

## Showing with Robert Oliver

*Is shoeing important in showing?*

Yes, very. The balancing of the foot and a neat, well shod foot is very important to many judges. At the Horse of the Year Show horses are assessed on a flat concrete surface and it is very important for a horse to be well shod and my winning horses have often won the best shod horse award as well.

*What is your type of show horse?*

Hacks, cobs, riding horses and hunters.

*What shoeing needs does it have?*

If a horse turns its toes in or out, corrective shoeing can make all the difference as can using the correct weight of shoe for the type of horse.

*What are the special demands of showing upon shoes?*

Horses need to be well shod to withstand hard and soft ground, galloping, twisting and turning. The hunter needs to be shod with medium-weight shoes whereas the show hack would need a set of light steel.

*Are there any particular problems you have with shoeing?*

The risk of pulling off a shoe either in work or whilst turned

*Robert Oliver.*

out in the paddock. Many show horses and ponies spread or pull a shoe whilst travelling thus running the risk of standing on it and puncturing their sole. This is more of a problem than people realise and it does not seem to matter how good the farrier is. It has happened to us twice with a champion this season.

*Do you prefer light shoes?*
Yes, but not plates as they are easily spread and we always use a stronger shoe behind.

*Have you ever used aluminium or glue-on shoes?*

Not glue-on, but wide aluminiums are used occasionally in front. Quite a number of showing people use aluminiums but no road work can be done and they do tend to spread.

*Do you prefer hot or cold shoeing?*

We have both and find them equally satisfactory.

*Do your horses wear their shoes out?*

Our show horses do only limited road work so they tend to have one new set and one set of removes.

*Can shoeing make a difference to your success?*

Yes. All our horses are shod regularly every three or four weeks and we take great care of their feet and shoeing.

*Have you ever had a bad experience with shoes?*

Yes, several. Probably the worst thing is for a horse to lose one just prior to a class, or arriving at a show having lost it travelling. Hot shoeing a day or two before a show with a thin-soled horse, the horse can then be lame the next day and often for a week or two.

# Racing with Martin Pipe

*Is shoeing important in racing?*

Yes. The horses must have a shoe to act on the surface to stop them slipping and to stop the foot breaking up on hard going, and the weight of the shoe is important.

*Martin Pipe.*

*What are your types of race horse?*

Flat and National Hunt horses.

*What shoeing needs do they have?*

'No foot — no horse'. Well fitted shoes for roadwork and light plates for racing.

*What are the special demands of racing upon shoes?*

Horses like humans need fitted shoes for correctness of speed. Calkins are very necessary to give horses grip and confidence on bends and over obstacles.

*Are there any particular problems you have with shoeing?*

It is very expensive.

*Do you prefer aluminium or steel shoes?*

Stainless steel for roadwork and aluminium for racing because they are lighter. This allows the horse more movement and is less dangerous for any over-reaches and cuts.

*Have you ever used glue-on shoes?*

Yes, they are very helpful with a soft foot.

*Do you prefer hot or cold shoeing?*

We use cold shoeing. Our shoes are made to fit the horse. Hot shoeing could make a thin-soled horse lame.

*Do your horses wear their shoes out?*

Yes, when they do a lot of roadwork.

*Can shoeing make a difference to your success?*

Yes, if a horse loses a plate. My horses are not allowed to run.

on three plates, so a lost shoe could cost the horse the race. A well-shod horse is less prone to tendon strain.

*Have you ever had a bad experience with shoes?*

Only perhaps when a shoe comes off in the stable at night and punctures a horse's foot preventing the horse from running.

*Mobile farrier Ron Clarke of Uxbridge, 1994.*

# CHAPTER 9

# YOU AND YOUR FARRIER

## Blacksmiths and Farriers

The meaning of the word farrier has changed over the years. Two hundred years ago a farrier was an animal doctor and did not shoe horses. Shoeing horses was carried out by the village blacksmith along with other ironwork. Then when animal doctors began to get properly trained and educated they started to call themselves veterinary surgeons. Some blacksmiths began to specialise in shoeing horses and called themselves shoeing smiths or farriers.

At the present time a farrier is defined as someone engaged in shoeing horses and a blacksmith is someone who does ironwork. Farriery is a trade by itself, and so is blacksmithing. However many do both and farriers are commonly referred to as black-smiths (though they may not like it very much).

## Training

Shoeing horses is a very skilled job and if wrongly done can cause a horse pain and injury. If anyone can learn the trade in a few years he or she will have done well. In Great Britain qualified farriers have undergone a four year apprenticeship, studied at college and passed a final examination. Proper training is essential if horses are to be given the standard of shoeing that horseowners demand and expect.

# Registration

The Farriers' Registration Act makes it unlawful for anyone except a vet to shoe a horse unless he or she is in the Register of Farriers. This Act was passed in 1975 to prevent horseshoeing by unskilled persons. Before this time anyone could call themselves a farrier and shoe horses with no guarantee of competence. Anyone who was working as a farrier at the time of the Act was allowed to register but only fully trained farriers are now allowed to do so.

At the time of writing there is a possibility that the Act might be repealed. It would be a tragedy for horse welfare if this were to happen.

# Qualifications

DWCF   the Diploma of the Worshipful Company of Farriers is the basic qualification that demonstrates competence to shoe horses.

AWCF   the Associateship of the Worshipful Company of Farriers demonstrates an ability to make a variety of surgical shoes.

FWCF   the Fellowship of the Worshipful Company of Farriers is the highest qualification for a farrier and demonstrates a fuller understanding of the uses of surgical shoes as well as an ability to make them.

*Horseshoeing at Stanford in the Vale, Berkshire, circa 1931.*

# Facilities

It used to be the case that every village had a blacksmith's forge. Horses would all be taken to their local forge to be shod. This was a good system as no-one had far to travel, the facilities were custom built and everything needed was to hand.

When the motor car took over from the horse as the main means of transport and the tractor took away the horses' work on the land the number of horses dropped dramatically and the village blacksmith lost most of his horseshoeing business.

Forges became few and far between and it became normal for farriers to travel to visit horses at their stables. This was, and is, less satisfactory because the conditions provided are rarely comparable to those at a purpose built forge with a shoeing area.

*Horseshoeing at Claverdon, Warwickshire, circa 1936.*

To make up for the lack of a proper working area it became normal for the travelling farrier to cold shoe horses in their stables. Under these cramped and gloomy conditions, however, it was not surprising that standards of shoeing dropped.

While some farriers made the effort to carry a portable coal fire around with them there were drawbacks with the time and mess involved. When portable propane gas forges were developed it became much easier to shoe horses hot under mobile conditions. However the lack of adequate shoeing areas is still the main limitation on the standard of shoeing.

To shoe a horse safely and well a clean dry floor is the first requirement. It is all very well working in a field when the ground is dry but it becomes a nightmare when the rain turns the ground to mud. Thus a concrete driveway with plenty of room for a van and for a horse to stand on is the least that should be provided. This is very satisfactory in good weather but to cope with bad weather a roof is necessary to provide shelter for horse and farrier from both rain and hot sun. The reason that so many old village forges had a chestnut tree outside was that the trees were planted to give shade from the hot summer sun.

The roof of the shelter must be high enough so that the horse will not hit its head even if it should rear up. The doors should be large enough so that a van can be backed up to it and still leave ample room for horses to be led in and out. There should be good light both natural and artificial. The temptation to clutter the place up with vehicles, machinery, show jumps and other odds and ends should be resisted. The shoeing area will also be useful for activities such as clipping, veterinary examinations and general grooming.

An empty stable is often the only shelter provided. For shoeing a horse there should be a wall ring in the opposite corner to the door. This will give the farrier easy access to either side of the horse. Poor light is the worst problem in a stable. A single light in the middle of the roof is inadequate because there will be a great deal of shadow cast by the horse itself. A better position for a single light is above the door. White painted walls improve the light levels enormously.

Fire is always a risk when hot shoeing and any obvious dangers like hay and straw should not be stored near the shoeing area. Shredded paper sometimes used as bedding is particularly easily ignited.

# Handling

The horse should have been brought in, the legs washed and dried and the feet picked out. Nothing makes the farrier's job more difficult and unpleasant than wet and muddy legs and feet. The hooves should not be oiled before shoeing because hoof oil makes the feet slippery and awkward to handle.

It is very desirable for the owner to be present when their horse is shod. Ideally horses should be held to be shod.

Many horses are happy to be tied up but this should be at the owner's risk. It must be remembered that horses might be startled and pull back on the rope. It is best not to tie the lead rope directly to a wall ring but to a single-strand loop of baler twine which will break if a horse panics. There should be no access to roads or wide open spaces if a horse does get loose.

Shoeing is not a painful process and most horses accept it very well and are very relaxed while being shod. Restlessness when it does occur can come from many reasons. The herd instinct is an important factor. Other horses being moved or fed can upset a horse. A horse may become distressed if taken away from its companions, or if its companions are taken away while it is being shod. This can easily be avoided by a little forethought.

*Horseshoeing at Thursley, Surrey, 1993.*

Many horses will put up a display of awkwardness especially when being shod for the first time or by a new farrier. They are just testing the situation to see what they can get away with and to see what kind of a reaction they can create. It is usually best for owner and farrier to take no notice of the horse's showing off and it will soon get bored and give up. Over-reacting will usually make things worse, and a horse will sense a nervous owner and play up all the more.

Hitting a horse should by and large be avoided. A nervous horse will only be made worse if hit. A horse which is being deliberately naughty or bites or kicks may be brought to its senses by a smack with the hand behind the shoulder or on the belly.

Flies are a particular nuisance during the summer and it is as well to be in the shade and to have a good supply of insect repellent handy and to bandage the horse's tail so that it does not swish in the farrier's face.

If a horse is proving very difficult to shoe then the best course of action is to call your veterinary surgeon to administer a sedative injection. Modern sedatives are so effective and safe that there can be no excuse for struggling with a horse that is a danger to itself, to the farrier and to everyone present.

# Relationships

Unreliability is perhaps the commonest complaint of horse owners directed at farriers. This is usually because farriers take on too much. Many owners do not always appreciate the special skills and education of farriers and have not been taught to recognise good horseshoeing. Nor do they realise the time and energy that goes into shoeing a horse well. The result is that farriers are rewarded for the quantity of work they do, not the quality. A better understanding will help owners to value their farriers and reward good work so that horses can be shod to the highest possible standard.

# Communication

The great advantage of being present, at least for part of the time, when your horse is shod, is that it allows any problems you or the horse are having to be discussed. Your farrier should be pleased to give advice and to do what he can to meet your requirements. It makes the job more rewarding if customers are interested in what a farrier is doing and show appreciation of his or her efforts. It also gives the opportunity to pay for the shoeing and to make the next appointment.

# Appointments

Another responsibility of the owner is to make sure that the horse is shod regularly; in most cases this means every six weeks. If a horse is doing a lot of work or has problem feet it may need to be shod more often. An appointment should be made for the next time after each shoeing. This way the shoes are changed before the hooves grow too long or shoes are lost and the hooves will stay in the best possible condition. The owner does not have to worry that he or she might not be able to get an appointment in a hurry and does not have to worry that the horse will not be available to be used at any given time. If a horse is being shod on such a regular basis most farriers are happy to replace any lost shoes which do occur at nominal cost.

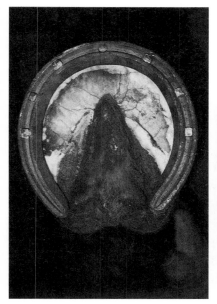

*A well shod riding horse.*

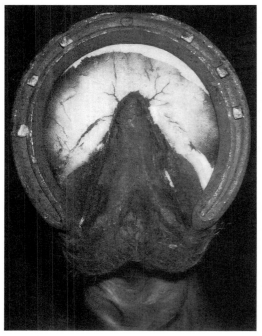 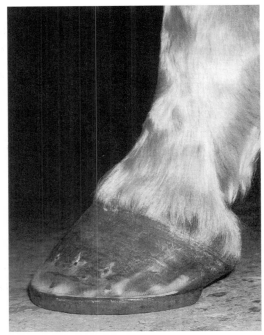

*A well shod hunter.*

## Lost Shoes

All horses lose shoes from time to time. If shoes are a poor fit and not nailed on well they are more likely to come off, but there are other reasons which cannot be entirely blamed on the farrier.

The commonest reason is an over-reach when a hind shoe catches the heel of a front shoe. Some horses have actions which predispose to over-reaching but any horse can do it especially when it gallops wildly around a field or slips about in muddy ground. Another is a tread when a horse stands on the edge of a shoe with the opposite foot. A third is spreading when a horse stamps the toe of a back foot on the ground and bends the shoe. Hind shoes that are stronger or have toe clips are needed for a horse which is prone to spreading.

Every horse has its quirks and it takes time and some trial and error for a farrier to find out the best way to shoe each individual animal to keep lost shoes to a minimum.

The soundness of the horse should always be the first priority. Extreme measures to avoid losing shoes, such as putting on shoes that are too small, will damage the foot. It is better to accept losing shoes occasionally rather than the alternative of lameness associated with corns or navicular disease, the result of short or close-fitting shoes.

# Lameness

Acts of farriery should not make a horse lame, even slightly or temporarily. However, everybody makes mistakes and, particularly when dealing with problem feet, it can sometimes happen that a horse will be sore after shoeing. It is important to discuss this with the farrier when it does happen so that he can take any action necessary to relieve the situation and will be able to avoid the same pitfall next time around.

# Veterinary Treatment

The diagnosis and treatment of disease or injury in animals is restricted to those who have the appropriate training, namely veterinary surgeons. Farriers cannot and should not do more than render first aid without the express direction of a veterinary surgeon.

# Surgical Shoeing

Many farriers who are very competent at everyday shoeing are not knowledgeable or experienced when it comes to surgical shoeing. If you think that your horse has a problem that might benefit from special shoeing you should consult your veterinary surgeon who will take on the responsibility for prescribing what is required and the responsibility for any difficulties that may arise.

The veterinary surgeon has great skill and knowledge but in most cases has little practical training in farriery. The best results come when the veterinary surgeon explains and discusses problems with the farrier.

# The Future

Some farriers have been reluctant to explain the technical details of what they are doing, perhaps because they did not want to leave themselves open to criticism. There is no need to pretend that horseshoeing is a hard and difficult job, because that is exactly what it is. Only by being open and ready to explain will the horseshoer find that his work will be appreciated. Only by understanding the basics of farriery will the horseman or woman be entitled to expect the best hoof care for their horses.

# INDEX